Lone Star Heart

Lone Star Heart
Poems of a Life in Texas

Michael Baldwin

LITERARY PRESS
LAMAR UNIVERSITY

ISBN: 978-1-942956-14-3
Library of Congress Control Number: 2016936030

Paintings: Johnny Bowen
Manufactured in the United States

Lamar University Literary Press
Beaumont, TX

Dedicated to all Texans who have nurtured Texas'
freedom, its friendliness, and its natural beauty.

Poetry from Lamar University Literary Press

Bobby Aldridge, *An Affair of the Stilled Heart*
Charles Behlen, *Failing Heaven*
Alan Berecka, *With Our Baggage*
David Bowles, *Flower, Song, Dance: Aztec and Mayan Poetry*
Jerry Bradley, *Crownfeathers and Effigies*
Jerry Bradley and Ulf Kirchdorfer, editors, *The Great American Wise Ass Poetry Anthology*
Matthew Brennan, *One Life*
Paul Christensen, *The Jack of Diamonds is a Hard Card to Play*
Christopher Carmona, Rob Johnson, and Chuck Taylor, editors, *The Beatest State in the Union*
Chip Dameron, *Waiting for an Etcher*
William Virgil Davis, *The Bones Poems*
Jeffrey DeLotto, *Voices Writ in Sand*
Mimi Ferebee, *Wildfires and Atmospheric Memories*
Larry Griffin, *Cedar Plums*
Ken Hada, *Margaritas and Redfish*
Michelle Hartman, *Disenchanted and Disgruntled*
Michelle Hartman, *Irony and Irreverence*
Katherine Hoerth, *Goddess Wears Cowboy Boots*
Lynn Hoggard, *Motherland*
Gretchen Johnson, *A Trip Through Downer, Minnesota*
Ulf Kirchdorfer, *Chewing Green Leaves*
Laozi, *Daodejing*, tr. By David Breeden, Steven Schroeder, and Wally Swist
Janet McCann, *The Crone at the Casino*
Erin Murphy, *Ancilla*
Laurence Musgrove, *Local Bird*
Dave Oliphant, *The Pilgrimage, Selected Poems: 1962-2012*
Kornelijus Platelis, *Solitary Architectures*
Carol Coffee Reposa, *Underground Musicians*
Jan Seale, *The Parkinson Poems*
Steven Schroeder, *the moon, not the finger, pointing*
Carol Smallwood, *Water, Earth, Air, Fire, and Picket Fences*
Glen Sorestad *Hazards of Eden*
W.K. Stratton, *Ranchero Ford/ Dying in Red Dirt Country*
Wally Swist, *Invocation*
Jonas Zdanys (ed.), *Pushing the Envelope, Epistolary Poems*
Jonas Zdanys, *Red Stones*

For information on these and other Lamar University Literary Press books go to www.lamar.edu/literarypress

Acknowledgments

I am grateful to the editors of these journals and anthologies for publishing some of the poems in this book.

Canis Latran
Illya's Honey
Louisiana Literature
Mutabilis Press Anthology
Red River Review
Scapes
Texas Poetry Calendar
Touchstone
Amarillo Bay

Other Books by Michael Baldwin

A Slam Poetry Manual
Scapes
Counting Backward From Infinity
Murder Music
Passing Strange

CONTENTS

Part I: Texas Weather

Part II: Texas Places

Part III: Texas Critters

Part IV: Texas Folks

Paintings

Part I
Texas Weather

Gonna Be a Hot One

Gonna Be A Hot One!

Many a Texas ranch has a dilapidated barn
with a corrugated iron roof that,
even though the day's barely begun,
already shimmers with heat waves
and groans complaintively as the rust hots up,
waking the red wasps nesting in its rafters
to buzz out and patrol their harsh domain
of Goat-Head, Bull-Nettle, Purple Thistle,
and grotesque green Osage Oranges
(uneaten since the giant ground sloth went extinct
twenty millennia ago) freshly fallen from
the bois d'arcs along the fence line,
vainly oozing thick sticky syrup in the sun,
where only Prickly Pear actually revel in the heat,
blooming extravagantly for desultory bees.
Yes, it's gonna be a hot one!

Dry Lightning

tears the air asunder—
a too-bright, jagged crack of light—
then the thunder,
blundering among flat-topped Texas hills,
announcing the arrival
of a green-black grumbler,
turning day to darkness,
roiling and rumbling,
threatening and promising,
but then passing, unpausing,
carrying an entire lake of water
elsewhere tonight,
leaving us somehow
unworthy of its wet blessing.

North Texas Summer

This summer has been brutally
normal for North Texas.
Two rainless, searing months
with thermometers stretching
their mercury thin as slug slime
up into the hundreds.
Only the grasshoppers seem
enthusiastic in their prospects.
My silver maple's spring-sprung
crop of fresh plump leaves
has divested in a dry cotillion.
The few remaining, withered,
wizened, cruelly disfigured, yet
cling with tenacious defiance.
As I watch, one leaf, large and grotesque,
succumbs, glides serenely
on the dragon's breath,
over the back fence, with the demeanor
of an immolated saint assumed to heaven.

Riding Out To Check The Pipes
Palo Pinto Lake, North Central Texas

Like frozen fists,
rough cumuli wreak
the weakened light,
bruise the sullen sky.
A few wild raindrops
stipple the windshield's
dusty transparency,
struggle erratically
to the wiper's margin mark,
surrender, then, and ride
its curve away into the dark.

Jagged geometries
of wind-worn stone,
Picassoesque masses
we pass among,
in chill *chiaroscuro*
of leaden light,
these morning hills
seem mourning night.

The lake lies shivering
in its canyon,
colder than an open coffin,
colder, still, remembering
how last summer we swam
in it so often.

The vacant house protests
too much with brittle
creaks and groans:
an old man too early
waked with winter
in his bones.

In folding back
the shuttered front
of the cast-iron
Franklin stove,
I find a stiffened

16

flicker's corpse
and take it gently
on my glove.

The bird attests
with grotesque grace,
when harsh unwelcome
it had found,
an adamantly unstoic death.
What stubborn spirit
here unbound?

Endless Forms

Threnody In Winter

Walking in the piney woods after
visiting the Houston Holocaust Museum

The gaunt moon makes its cold nest in the wind—
A grumpy toad hunkers in a lost summer shoe—
late daisies limp into winter on toothless unicycles—
Sandhills bow the sky, croaking southlessly—
A sweet gum's yellow star presses to my chest,
then desperately rejoins the leaf storm—
A few new mushrooms struggle bravely up
through decayed manure like naked children—
Skeletal trees, ensnarled by thorn vines,
frighten even the sparrows—
An abandoned burn pile, still smoldering,
exhales smoke flows like writhing shadows—
Pine cone cantatas whisper *"Dies Irae,"*
song of death on the Day of Wrath,
as they scatter thousands of tiny
dead angels' wings—
Now the woods, the wind, the birds are silent—
Soon it will rain,
the rain of forgetting—
Nor will the wind remember—
But the earth—
The earth will always know the truth.

Blue Norther, Downtown Fort Worth

Glaucous clouds shiver on
      Commerce's dark mirrors,
glassy glaciers, freezing the sun's
      last glister, cast it
wanly down among desolate
      concrete chasms where wolf-wind
prowls, slavers leaves and litter
      at our legs, howls up alleys.
Skinny street trees, all blown bare,
      no more autumn-elegant,
scratch the air with fierce futility
      at the tear-wind's taunt.
Winter's first Norther has caught
      many without coats.

A scatter of sparrows,
      dark rain upon gaunt limbs,
bleak branches streaked white,
      the stain unhid by
feathered foliage, by countless
      bird-years, perching.
And some will fall frozen tonight,
      numbed by habit
before cold, and, if not
      a sparrow falls unknown,
yet falls and dies, alone.

Leaf Laughter

Harris County

Elms and oaks and Tupelos
unleaving, ungrieving,
undressing tree tresses,
confessing with colors their
seasonal sin.
Leaf laughter comes after
quitting their day jobs.
Dancing while dying,
the leaves keep on trying,
seducing the wind,
their ramble and scramble
and gambol extend.
We without winter
fill five months with Autumn.
For leaves that's a lifetime
they would not rescind.

Wind

North Texas is notorious for its winds.
As a tennis player, I'm particularly
sensitive about wind conditions.
Playing tennis during high school years,
we seldom had wind screens on the courts.
So often we'd play in breezes that made
getting the ball over the net or just keeping it
on the court a feat of strength, skill, and strategy.
Those were mere zephyrs, however.
Stronger gales are frequent visitors in these parts.
Vicious straight-line winds that often precede
storms, hereabouts, can knock down barns and fences.
Windmills have disconnects or they would spin off
their derricks in a typical stout Texas gale.
West Texas now takes pride in its horrific dust storms,
since most everything there has been blown elsewhere.
Then there's the twisters that can be seen swooping
down and grooving paths of torment across the plains,
careening like demons, sometimes in multiples,
roaring like a thousand freight trains conflagrating,
mesmerizing and terrorizing children watching
from doomed trailer parks or cracker box '50's houses.
No wonder one of the early classic novels of Texas
was titled *The Wind*, and detailed the progressive
insanity of its heroine, blown to suicide by its incessancy.
But there must be something fascinating or challenging
about our winds, because we Texans mostly just
hunker down here and refuse to be blown away.

Stock Show Parade

Back then, as now, the Fort Worth Rodeo
and Fat Stock Show was held in January.
I guess they figured the animals could tolerate
the cold better than the heat. At any rate,
the Stock Show Parade in which I marched
was usually accompanied by a bitter Blue Norther.

Waiting by the Courthouse for the parade to begin,
we're glad for the thick wool
of our high school band uniforms
that were so stifling last summer.
We play *"El Capitan"* as we march in place
awaiting our turn to enter the parade,
cursing the hundreds of horses that preceded us,
littering the street in their passing.
The horses clomping in front of us snort out
gouts of vapor, and their iron hoofs ring like bells
against the frozen bricks of Throckmorton.
Now we join the parade,
blasting out *"The Thunderer"* and breaking
our eight to five stride only
to avoid the steaming horse piles
that seem so strategically placed.

One of the trumpets rips his lips
on his frozen mouthpiece,
keeps playing though, blowing blood
from his spit valve at each pause in the music.
We're blaring *"Semper Fidelis"* when
the bass drummer skips a beat to whack at
the stallion that has sauntered through the ranks
to nibble the drummer's hat plume.
The young cowgirl rider finally regains
control of the nag, and we march away,
minus a few feathers, to the strains of *"Colonel Bogey."*

My fingers are now too numb to play my clarinet,
so I just hold on and fake it.
But the corks have shrunk in the cold
and suddenly the whole bottom half
simply falls away through my unfeeling fingers.

How lucky can you get!
Instead of shattering on the concrete street,
the ebony bell has found a huge horse pile
to nestle into and is rescued
by the cute flutist marching behind me.

Now I bless those beautiful horses
as we stomp on down Houston Street
with *"The Stars and Stripes Forever"*
blazing patriotic warmth into the frigid,
fantastic, horse-prancing, crowd-shouting,
flag-waving, wild-Westing, Cowtown,
Yahoo!, rodeo air.

Part II: Texas Places

Upland Jewels

Chisos Splendor
Big Bend

We call them Adam's needle,
Giant Dagger, Spanish Bayonet,
and simply Yucca (its Indian name).
The species inhabiting Texas'
Chisos Mountains are particularly
formidable in this country so arid
and sun-battered.

Among these far mountains
and mesas, boulders and buttes,
Yucca give a thrusting brutal beauty
to a vista of thirsty distance.
In this ecology of bleak fecundity,
Yucca, Big Bend Blue Bonnets,
Desert Marigolds, and Purple Sage
compete not for sunlight, but for water.
So Yucca send tap roots down
hundreds of feet for moisture,
then guard it with sharpness.

In summer, thousands of white flower
bells attract thousands of white moths
that couple the Yucca and bed their eggs
in balls of golden pollen to hatch within
the Yucca's seed pods; a marriage of
mutual necessity between insect and plant.
A mystery and a wonder.

If we could view this scene with God's eye,
we would see the energy of light
becoming the energy of life
in a vast complexity of harmony in diversity,
of extravagance in extremity,
of grace in grim circumstance.
Art is God's eye,
dauntless as Yucca's dagger.

Enchanted Rock

You are the deep, hard heart of Texas,
beating with a billion-year pulse.
Bursting from granite bones
to sing of Earth's deep agony,
to offer yourself for human reverence,
to teach the deep mysteries of spirit.
How many Tonkawa, Apache, Comanche
still haint your blood-pinked stone,
are heard singing their death chants
invisibly, crackling with agony
as the rock cools with evening?
And are these bats or restless spirits
that come swarming, keening hungrily
from your deep cavities at dusk?
How many stars have pricked the darkness
to watch your ghosts dance upon this dome?
How many hot moons have rasped
along your rim to guide the way to other realms?
How many harsh lives have you harrowed
in man's mere twelve thousand years here?
Your stone is stained with blood and spirit,
and yet your deep, hard heart has beat only once.

Encounter

Texas Hill Country

A fallen sycamore
in cerements of moss
across our path
insisted that we sit,
watch the day moon
mount the inner sphere,
traversed, too,
by the languorous spiral
of a Red-Tailed Hawk.
Tranced eyes released,
we found ourselves observed:
ten feet away
a white-tail doe
(so still my mind ignored
at first my eye);
curiosity complete, she snuffed
and slowly deliquesced
among the trees.
Where are such easy certainties
of these feral things in us?

Prickly Pears

Llano Estacado

Why write about blankness?
The "Palisaded Plains" Coronado called them.
But when he reached the top of this tableland,
he saw no landmarks to navigate by,
no trees or brush or boulders;
too high to see horizon.
It was an utter emptiness to desolate the soul.
More recent travelers say it is 85 percent sky.
This high desert became the last refuge
of Comanche pursued by foolhardy cavalry
into this harsh, thirsty emptiness.
Unknowing, they rode over the largest
underground lake in the world: the *Ogallala*,
laid down by glaciers two million years ago,
and hidden till deep wells could be drilled
thru the hard cap rock to claim these plains
for cotton farms and Baptist churches.
Yucca knew there was moisture here.
Only it could send taproots down
hundreds of feet to sip that ancient water.
Perhaps the stumps of yucca were
what caused some to translate *Estacado*
as the "staked" plains, since these were
the only markers on the otherwise featureless prairie.
When the *Ogallala* is gone
(drunk dry for desiccated dollars),
the *Llano* will again be vacant of life.
Double empty; even the Yucca will vanish.
Desocupado, vacio, vacante.
Who will care to rename it?

Camping Palo Duro Canyon

The Lighthouse hoodoo broods
Sphinxlike in the gathering twilight.
The campfire, in what shall be
its shallow grave, is not yet ready
to expire. Red and yellow flames
still lick at limbs among the ashes.
But now bright embers outnumber
the flickering dancers that scatter
skittering shadows upon the prairie,
mysterifing all the ordinary
implements and occupants
of its shrinking circumambience.
Stars, like campfire sparks reflected
by the sky's dark mirror, form
bright hordes in stop-action stampede.
The embers bend back the night,
then succumb to its enticement,
finally to find their cozying,
warm beneath their own ashen blanket,
waiting to be bestirred for breakfast.

Alamony

When I was in sixth grade, in 1956,
Texas history was conveyed by a strange pedagogy.
Each child was given a thick comic book titled
Texas History Movies. It was visually thrilling
with color pictures of dramatic stories from Texas history
in horizontal strip panels like regular comics.
I recently learned that Texas History Movies
was originally published in the Dallas Morning News
in 1926 specifically for use in the schools.
They were called "movies" because the strips were likened
to images on movie film transferred to paper.
These comics were reprinted in many editions and formats
between the '20's and about 1960, and have been revised
and republished sporadically since.
Because they were printed on cheap paper and were primarily
owned by school children, few of the early copies remain.

I was inspired by my THM to do my own drawing
of the Battle of the Alamo in extravagant detail.
It would undoubtedly have launched me into a career
as a major artist had not my 6th grade teacher caught me
working on it during math, destroyed it, and embarrassed me
in front of the class. I haven't been able to draw
a recognizable figure since. But, as they say,
when God closes a door, He opens a window.
I defenestrated myself thru that metaphorical window
to become a writer (after failing to become a jazz clarinetist,
a pro tennis player, an astronaut, and a lawyer).

After the fiasco with the drawing, I was leery
of all things Alamo, and even resisted its allure when
my family visited San Antonio during my teen years.
It was only as an adult, and quite by accident, that I came
to appreciate the true significance of the Alamo
to Texans and to humanity.

I was in San Antonio attending a professional conference
one summer, when, having stayed out late with friends
on the River Walk and having consumed a few libations,
I decided to walk back to my hotel alone.
San Antonio's streets, rather than being laid out

in a rational grid pattern, are instead governed by
the inebriate wanderings of the San Antonio River.
This can cause considerable confusion to one who
is unfamiliar with the city, and perhaps guided
by spirits (liquid and otherwise) himself.
Thus, erroneously but fatefully I found my way
to the Alamo rather than my hotel.

It was after midnight; the summer air was redolent
of honeysuckle, and opulent with moonlight;
the plaza was empty; the walls of the Alamo
were cool and somehow welcoming
as I leaned confusedly against them.
Then my body began to tingle electrically
and I seemed to merge into that limestone mass
as if into a mother's bosom, as my soul itself
succumbed, surrendered to the spirit of the Alamo.
I saw not visions of battle, nor of Bowie, Crockett, Travis,
but rather was suffused with a great, serene sadness,
and with a sense of the dignity of death, not welcomed
but accepted Stoically as necessary and meaningful,
of self-determined, undespairing death,
of death that held no horror, but rather the sanctity
of souls struggling toward blessedness.
I leaned long into those haunted walls,
waiting, wanting to be completely
absorbed into their sacred immensity,
to share the enormity of their being.
Then, finally, sober, yet still trembling
with its sublime vibrations,
I made my way away from the Alamo
carrying its fierce melancholy within me,
and have never needed to return.

Those Texas Stars

"The stars at night are big and bright,
Deep in the heart of Texas." —June Hershey

Surely star-spun—man's imagination.
Had clouds eternally obscured the stars,
our curiosity, perhaps all higher thought,
would have languished also in those clouds.
It was the stars, themselves, in the vast night
of Earth's Pleistocene, that fired the mind
of early man to set us reaching for our higher selves.

Teening up in the 60's, I wanted to be a scientist,
followed NASA's agonies and attainments,
read science and science fiction voraciously,
and built my own Newtonian telescope,
with which I drank the stars to drunkenness.

Nowanights, most people seldom see the stars.
Light pollution from electric lumination
obscures the grandeur of the night sky
so few now understand the importance
of the stars to human history, to man's destiny.

There are few high wildernesses left in Texas
where sufficient dark allows us to appreciate
the forms and fires of the immense above.
Behemoth machine eyes of McDonald Observatory
nightly mine and magnify ancient starlight,
photons flung this way millennia past, so
we may analyze their light to learn their age, size,
distance, temperature, composition, motion, relations,
and even if they have planets on which beings
as curious as we, may be watching, wondering, imagining.

Coyotes moan among the bleak Davis Mountains,
as crisp night air conspires with natural darkness
to allow the stars in their billions to display
their glory, and to once again fire the imagination
of at least one puny human.

Ancient Sentinel

Upon This Rock

Palo Pinto Lake, North Central Texas

Before this rill
was blocked and filled
the rocks that populate these hills
were desiccate and monochrome.
Now the lake beyond itself
extends a moist embrace
that makes these sandstone
boulders bloom with varicolored colonies
of lichen, like living Pollock paintings:
stippled, splashed, hue-bestrewn.

A mosswork quilt envelopes each
vulnerable, benign giant,
deflecting the force
of wind's and rain's erosion—
a symbiosis of hard haven
and soft armor.
Like sentinels of some ancient
chthonic race they await perhaps
a signal forgotten even by the hills.
The trees ascend and sink about them
over eons in a ragged respiration.
And we are but flickers of light (or less)
at the corners of their consciousness.

Upon this rock I have lain
naked as a lizard,
Zen empty mind attempted,
cool moss combining with my cheek,
and heard the boulder's spirit speak
in deep slow whispers
in its sleep and mine.
And merged myself so with its being
we became a single organism,
dual anachronism,
a passive, encompassing perception,
at once aware of beetles burrowing
our lichen hair,
the tread of mastodon and deer,

of mountains, glaciers, oceans splashed
with light, and gleams of dreaming
galaxies lost in the lake of night.

Formosa Garden Guitar

Cognitive dissonance in San Antonio

Hot and sour soup—just acceptable.
Snow peas et al—unexceptional.
Garlic shrimp—requires more Hunan heat.
White china, white rice, white
noise of conversation. Then, unexpectedly,
refreshingly, a lovely Latina guitarist strums
ardent jazz melodies into aural interstices,
juking on Django and moaning a *Malaguena*,
insinuating sinuous rhythms among clinking dishes,
scattering pungent sonic spices.
The oolong now seems more fragrant.
Tree ears curl in delight upon the plate.
The cuisine becomes superb because
the guitar is delicious.

Once Upon A Time In Austin

1967-68 were the best worst years of my life.
I arrived in Austin in the aftermath of UT's
tower sniper murders of 16 people,
the first major instance of gun terror in the US.
I moved to Austin to attend law school,
not because I particularly wanted
to be a lawyer, but because friends
were there, I had scraped by on the LSAT,
and the Vietnam War was devouring
those without college or other deferments.

Austin then was a paradise for footloose youth,
Hippyness was in high spirits and high gear,
topless nudity was in vogue at Barton Springs,
where the water was so cold, you went
instantly numb and so didn't find it unpleasant.
That cold was helpful when I stepped thru
an unseen beer bottle and severely cut
my foot. The frigid water kept the blood
from spilling till the cut was tourniqueted.

Fortunately the foot healed without
slowing me down, because my great
pleasure then was tennis, and my best
athletic attribute was my speed.
Newly married, my wife and I were befriended
by a local neurosurgeon who was also
a tennis fanatic. We played many mixed-
doubles matches with him and his nurse.
He would then take us poor students to local
restaurants where we would regale
the waiting line with barbershop quartet songs.
Somehow we always got a table quickly.
He was a wonderful conversationalist,
bon vivant, and generous friend.
After we moved back to Fort Worth,
he often flew his Piper up to play tennis.
He died tragically in a plane crash
at Austin airport two years after we left.

I nearly met the same fate while still in Austin.
A student-pilot friend offered to take me up
while he acquired a few flight hours.
My door popped open on the assent
and I couldn't close it until we leveled off.
Quite a view from halfway out of the plane!
We flew for several hours but encountered
a storm over Austin on our return.
We were shaken like dice in a cup by heavy winds.
The rain was so intense on the windshield
just inches from our eyes, we could see only doom.
Lightning seemed to seek us out. Somehow
we found a hole in the clouds to drop thru,
and made our way to the airfield flying low.
It was both terrifying and exhilarating.

Anticlimactically, law school was such a bore I
threw it over and returned to Fort Worth for a life
of literary adventure as a library administrator.
But my two years in Austin were among my most
memorable, perhaps simply because of my youth
and freedom in a city of national importance
(President Johnson called it home and visited often)
and Austin was a magnet of the national youth culture.

But 1968 was also the year both Martin Luther King
and Bobby Kennedy were assassinated.
It was the worst year of the Vietnam War,
with the highest casualties, the Pueblo Incident,
and the My Lai massacre. President Johnson
announced he would not seek reelection.
Thousands of French students rioted in Paris.
Russian tanks crushed the Prague Spring fling with democracy.
Arlo Guthrie débuted his antiwar anthem *Alice's Restaurant*.
The Democratic Party Convention in Chicago ended
with police rioting and beating peaceful demonstrators.
Richard Nixon was elected President,
but didn't end the war as he had promised.
The US sent the first manned mission to orbit the moon.
UT won the SW Conference and Cotton Bowl in 1968,
and, undefeated, won the national championship in 1969.
It was a time of horrors and wonders.
It was the time they mean when they say
"Keep Austin Weird!"

Gillette Farm Mallards

Gators of Caddo Lake

Caddo Lake, is replete with ambiguity.
No one is sure how it formed.
Perhaps by the earthquake of 1812,
or maybe by a natural logjam blockage
of the Red River, also in the early 1800's.
The Spanish and French couldn't decide
whom it belonged to, since it straddled
the border of both their territories.
It became a no-man's-land and a refuge
for outlaws and runaway slaves.
The closest town is named *Uncertain*.

But the lake is a natural wonder
and a Texas treasure.
We vacationed there some of my teenage summers.
A rustic cabin among pines, dogwood, redbud,
and willow sat near the shore and gave us
views of the many-footed cypress giants seeming
to wade within the swamp among lotus pods
thrust up on thick stalks with pure white petals.
Spanish moss hung like witch's hair
from every tree and havened congeries of birds,
my favorites being Painted Bunting, White Ibis,
Pileated Woodpecker, Yellow-Throated Warbler.

But it was critters in the water that interested me
even more than the birds. Alligators
glided the bayous like grim green ghosts.
At night we would sometimes hear a crowd
of male gators roaring like revving motorcycles
and slapping the water with their jaws
to impress the silent females.
One day at Caddo, I encountered
three different kinds of gator.

While rowing a canoe near the shore,
I noticed the movement of an empty
plastic milk jug attached to a trot line.
Pulling it up, I found a two-foot
Alligator Gar, a fearsome fish,
whose long thin snout of wicked teeth
had snarled in a tangle of fishing line.
I didn't see the four-foot Alligator
that wanted the gar for lunch.
The gator chomped the gar, body

from head, and nearly pulled me in
as I stupidly held onto the line.
I quickly gave way to the gator
and made for the lake shore.

Walking back to the cabin, I came upon
a maybe 50-pound Alligator Snapping Turtle
calmly ambling overland from one bayou
to the next and in no hurry at all it seemed.
Fascinated to find a snapper on land,
I came up close behind to view
the pattern of conical projections
on his mossy black-green carapace.
But as I approached, he suddenly
levitated several inches straight up,
whirled around to face me with a hissing
from his horrific hooked beak,
and came for me at a turtle's gallop.
I quickly vacated the vicinity,
leaving the snapper to his perambulation.
Three gators in an hour was quite enough
excitement to make me remember Caddo Lake
with no uncertainty for the rest of my life.

Xmas Epiphany

Downtown Houston, mid-December,
chill enough to spill a drizzle,
extravagant with gigawatts of neon,
argon, mercury vapor,
sodium, sulfur, chlorine phosphor,
pointillistic lumination,
miles of lights limn arrogant towers,
smearing spectral brightness on the night.
From far suburban sanctuaries
these must seem God's Christmas tree,
surely visible from space.
But down on near-deserted streets:
a lightmare, a crazy rain
of color-cursed photons
makes sickly shadows in a dozen directions.
The vacant, weird-lit misty plaza,
like an opening scene from some ghost opera.
Why was I startled, then, by your sudden
apparition as I emerged my cab?
You were thin and brown
as a lost sparrow's feather,
holding tightly to your trembling breast
the tiniest baby I had ever seen,
emaciated Madonna.
I was afraid you wanted to give me the child.
"Justa dolla mista; milk fo tha chile."
I could barely hear your whisper.
Those eerie lights reflected from your dark
eyes with a mesmeric intensity, not of anger or
demand but with an implacable dignity of need.
And I, cashless in my expensive suit, ashamed,
rebuffed you silently and slithered into the hotel.
Years later your beautiful, terrible eyes
still reproach me. Was it just
those mist-mad Christmas lights?

Peaceful Crossing

Stillness At Old Bosque Bridge

There is something in nature that wants perfect stillness.
Yes, water loves movement, loves to shimmer sunlight
in our eyes as it shivers down a streamway.
Air, too, is enamored with pushing clouds about
the big Texas sky and setting leaves atremble.
But nature finds some deep satisfaction
in the utter stillness of a moment's eon,
as when a Great Blue Heron, poising for a strike,
exactly echoes the arch
of an abandoned bridge over the Bosque River.
Even unseen stones, dreaming deep within
the river's dancing mind, become
some integral gestalt with all that's human-seen,
as nature meditates, contemplates in its totality,
in perfect stillness, the beauty it has created
for the human mind to appreciate,
or to ignore in our ignorant worldly strivings.

First Memory

A verdant glade with leaves in many
shades of green, luffing, lifting, shifting,
sorting sunlight through gently swaying
branches just above my head.
This is my earliest Memory.
Perhaps I lay upon a quilt
on a swath of grass on a summer's day
at Fort Worth's Botanic Gardens,
and, being a baby, could not much move my gaze,
so gazed amazed at never-before-seen greenery.
No people intrude into this evergreen memory;
it is serene and safe and yet mysteriously
immesmering to my infant mind.
Simple but subtly powerful, this first memory.
Did it somehow instill my life-long lure to nature?
Have I sought the source of that memory
my entire life, wanting to regain that infant's
sense of serenity and delight?
Why was that simple memory retained
when most others of my infancy
were erased in my brain's inexorable
pruning and retuning of its neurons?
Memories are subject to winnowing
by natural selection, as the brain evolves
in an individual, even as are species themselves.
That first green memory must have meant
more somehow than I may ever understand.
I wonder if, like HAL's forced retrospection
in 2001, A Space Odyssey, it will also be
the last thing I remember.

Ghost Town
Thurber, Texas

She found a sun-purpled medicine bottle,
hand-blown, from the late 1800's.
It was a good find; there were lots of shards,
but few whole objects left from decades
of people picking over Thurber's mostly bare
abandoned acres that had been neighborhoods,
businesses, ball fields, all the accouterments
of a once thriving North Texas town.

Thurber was something special.
It was the first self-contained company town
in the nation in the 1880's. It was built around
the only active coal mine in Texas.
It was a town of immigrants: Poles, Italians,
Mexicans, and many more lived and worked
harmoniously. It was the first fully electrified
town in the nation, with its own power plant.
Every house had running water and natural gas.
Thurber had its own opera house, hosting
some of the most famous singers of the times.
It had the largest ice house in the Southwest.

Thurber's business was to supply coal
to the Texas & Pacific Railway, which opened
the West to easy railway travel and commerce.
Thurber also had the largest brick making facility
west of the Mississippi. Its vitrified red bricks
paved the streets of many southern cities.
Fort Worth's Stockyards area is still distinctive
of the 1800's due to Thurber bricks, as is Austin's
Congress Avenue, and Galveston's seawall.

Oil was discovered near Thurber as WWI erupted.
This enabled America to join the war despite
newly Red Russia's cutting off oil to the Allies.
When the railroads shifted to oil-burning engines
in the 1920's, Thurber's coal industry
and the town, itself, were doomed.

Thurber still has its graveyard, and its tall
brick smokestack marks its persistence on I-20.
My wife's Italian father grew up in Thurber
so we often joined the annual reunion
of former residents from their diaspora.

Thurber embodied much of what Texas
was and is about: the opening and civilizing
of the West, the rapid pace of change,
the power of the human spirit to endure
and to keep moving forward,
the ability of many nationalities
to coexist together if given the chance.
I hope Thurber maintains its identity
and helps us remember its importance,
even if it remains a Texas ghost town.

Preludes

This chill, fall North Texas morning
I walk with Chopin.
Rubinstein, too, finds the crisp air bracing
for he plays the preludes with warm enthusiasm.
A few late wildflowers straggle along the roadside
sparse and small, yet courageously continuing to bloom.
The gaunt old chestnut mare, alone in her field,
nods not her usual greeting. Instead,
head over fence, she softly mutters
a vaporous invitation.
I stop to stroke her neck, her jaw,
and gaze into her chocolate eyes.
I have no treat this morning and she asks none.
But she stretches out her white blaze face
toward mine, beckoning, and I lean into her,
immersing my face in her velvet muzzle.
Her nostrils blow gently on my neck
and we commune for many moments.
Then, I realize that she, too, is listening
to Chopin, with quiet attentiveness.
The prelude ends;
her soft nose trembles and we part.
The next morning I bring Schubert
for the horse to hear.
But she lies dead in the field
(brown mound, crow-crowned),
used up with years and loneliness.
Perhaps she decided Chopin needed a horse.

Doodlebug & Friends

Halloween Day On Padre Island
For Emily, Jackson, and Eddie

Cold sun consumes morning mist,
creates a perfect autumn day for
walking the foaming, questing surf line
with trousers rolled above our knees,
bare feet licked lasciviously by sliding tides,
footprints sinking inches in wet grit, then
disappearing with each next inundation.
We search out shells of whelk and scallop,
luminous, translucent sea glass
(how many thousand tumblings to
scour smooth and make magical?),
and the hooked leather pouch of
a shark's dark, abandoned egg case.
My grandsons, seven and three,
view these treasures with innocent
inquisition, then look for more to make
me praise again their scanning skills,
and wade too far into the swallowing
surf, so their mother scolds
yet cannot deter their enthusiasm,
oblivious as yet to the tides
of ocean, of life, of time.

Steel Creek Sonata

Brazos River Nocturne

Nature makes music by night.
Darkness engages our ears and imagination
With melodious murmurs, symphonic
susurrations of water ripples rivering
among rocks, tree tongues set singing
by night breezes, insects, frogs,
and night birds blending in concert.

But always it is the moon
that enchants the night,
gliding among glowing clouds,
casting such etheric luminance
upon the water that all beings
become imaginary, become ghosts
of themselves, even our selves.

So, wading deer may be spirits
from an age before man,
manifesting when moonlight,
bent back into its own albedo
by moon's and water's mirrors,
becomes a sacred, timeless,
noctilucent, entranced
entrance for imaginings.

Thus the night mind
mothers our ancient children
and sings them lullaby.

Spring Tonic

Wildflower Witness
Texas Hill Country

A mild, wet winter caressed
the earth and spilled
the Texas hills with flowers.
Firewheels whirl,
set blazing crazily
by sun shafts reclaiming
fresh-washed prairie
from a wandering thunderhead.
Coneflowers,
in ardent yellow,
mock Coronado's *El Dorado*.
Prickly Pear
save their blooms for summer,
but Bluebonnets
in proud profusion,
like a convocation
of Daughters of the Texas Revolution,
gather reverently around the ruin,
a granite pioneer hearth
forgotten by all but
a pair of hoary oaks,
and spend themselves in beauty
for this itinerant witness.

Leaning Trees

Old dog and I amble a country road between
Conroe and Montgomery, between
a stand of Loblolly pines and a horse pasture.
The pines are scrawny and sick with beetles.
But a pair of Pileated Woodpeckers
find them delicious, hammering the trees
with long yellow beaks till the trunks tremble
their gratitude and dead bark divests in chunks.

We cut across the pasture toward home.
The only trees here are two long-limbed
Live Oaks leaning precariously,
embracing one another at perilous angles,
presser pressing pressee slowly, inexorably
horizontal, and, in that event, surely
assuring its own uprooting.
Is this a tango in infinite largo, the flyer
frozen in the moment of horizontal swoop?

The trees' extreme contortions
remind me too somehow of
Laocoon and the serpent.
But perhaps instead of a struggle,
it is a century-long seduction,
or maybe a Good Samaritan
supporting a wounded comrade
on a battlefield invisible to
the non-arboreal among us.

The acute lean of the support tree
makes a fine scratching surface
for the young Appaloosa that seems
the lone inhabitant the pasture.
He heeds not the danger of a deadfall
in his desire for a back rub.
Then he waters the tree in gratitude.

Old dog hesitates, then, inspired or
challenged by the colt, follows suit
with a hind-leg salute.

Sunset at Sam's Throne

Texas Underground

Texas Hill Country

We hiked up the Devil's Backbone, amid cactus,
    cone flowers, mesquite, and *pinyon* pines,
and found one firmly rooted near the precipice
    on which to belay our nylon lines.
Walked backward over the edge of the world
    and rappelled down its granite wall,
streaked with water's black calligraphy,
    and pocketed with tiny paradises of moss.
Found the mountain's secret ear, a slit
    mere inches wide but tall enough for us to fit.
And entered and descended still, like spiders
    spinneretting silk, and found the cave's
unfootmarked floor, some thirty feet below its door.
    And walked straight in some fifty more.
Encountered a wall, wet, riddled with cavities, rampant
    with salamanders like black-dappled sulfur,
feasting on crickets and dancing daddy longlegs.
    They politely ignore our brash curiosity.

Down the opposite passage the chamber narrows
    and descends. We light our carbide lanterns
and lock them to our hard-hats. The hissing flame illumines
    formations of popcorn, bacon rind, and soda straws.
Pushing the darkness before us, the lights swoop
    with each head turn, bounce with each step.
The passage narrows all around like walking down
    the inside of an ice-cream cone to its point.

And there we crawl, wriggling through an intestinal
    tunnel, resisting claustrophobia.
Emerging at last into a large room of rubble: boulders
    hunched like gargoyles, stalactites menacing us
from the ceiling like saber-toothed cats about to spring,
    massive draperies of calcium carbonate
sparkling with wetness, rippling seams of silver on white.
    And in the center of this sunken cathedral,
a pool of water so still, so transparent, it seems
    an invisible mirror, refractively flashing
our lights about the cave like silent lightning.

Within the pool two albino carp swim
in slow, serene circles, making not a ripple.
        Have they swum thus since time immemorial?

We stroke them with lights that make them iridess
        but they are blind and waver not
from the prescribed pattern of their eternal patrol.
        "Let's see the dark," we said. A caver's thrill;
few non-cavers ever see the absolute absence of light.
        Our eyes are not designed to cope with utter dark.
We snuff the lanterns and watch the dark appear,
        a darkness so intense the eye must invent light
where none exists to tolerate so great a nothingness.
        The dark presses our eyes so heavily
our retinas emit sparks like ghosts of fireflies past.
        And in that pressing, dancing darkness
we hear a sound where none should be. A sighing,
        a whispering, a susurration of the palpable dark.
There is a breeze as if the cave is breathing.
        Frightened, we quickly re-light our carbides.
The fish, too, are agitated, now swimming
        nervously, erratically, expectantly.
We see a trickle of water glistening along the floor
        where all was dry before.

We understand, now, and hurry back the way we came.
        Crawling recklessly through the narrow tunnel,
belly deep in water flowing like a stream against us
        and rising steadily. We abandon our back packs,
reach the mouth of the tunnel with just our heads
        above the torrent, and, finding higher ground,
hike quickly to where our ropes had hung.
        A waterfall now sprays from the cave's high mouth.
The spotted yellow salamanders on the wall watch us
        with pity and wriggle back into the rotten rock.
Desperate, we find a wall that can be free-climbed, then
        chimneyed, walking up one wall, backs against another.
And when we're nearly to the top we see the ropes
        thrashing in the water's spray.
Catching the ropes and snapping them to our karabiners,
        we climb the last few yards through gushing water.
Emerging from the cave into a blowing rainstorm

we scale the cliff and lie laughing like maniacs
on top of the mountain, muddy, bloody, stunned
with exhaustion, but exhilarated from
coming out alive after having counted coup
upon the stony face of troglodytic death

Blackberry Eden

Montgomery County, Texas

Suddenly globuled,
     like black holes gobbling
       their white dwarf flower stars,
wild blackberries,
     appear in profusion,
      catching us unprepared.
Yet, undeterred,
     we catch them, too,
      in bellied T-shirts,
and gorge,
     gashed vermilion
      staining fingers and faces.
Your long hair tangles
     in cat-clawed brangles,
      and you squeal
with only half-feigned fear,
     for here the copperhead
      is known to lair,
so, sweating
     in the danger-heavy air,
      your upper lip
glistening erotically
     in this impossible place,
      we dance
a chary bolero among the thorns,
     emerging written
      with their script
inscribed on abdomen and arms,
     carry off their dark treasure
      to feast upon at leisure,
and even dream
     the berries in our beds,
      taunted and entangled
by thorn fronds, each fruit
     an ebon panther's eye,
      eluding and alluring us
        into the labyrinth.
Days later we return

with buckets, but the berries
have all shriveled
to dark pinheads in the heat;
only bare, brown, angry canes remain,
skeletal stalks, still menacing,
yet, already aestivating.
Will it be the same with us?

Part III: Texas Critters

Mockingbird

I don't really quibble with the Mockingbird
being the State Bird of Texas, even though
Mockers are also the state bird of Arkansas,
Tennessee, Florida, and Mississippi.
And ironically for all these Dixieland states,
its full name is the Northern Mockingbird.
Blue Jays are more festively colored,
Red Tail Hawks are more magnificent,
Road Runners are more indicative
of Texas prairies and dry plains.
Texas Turkey Vultures remind us
of how the State Legislature operates.
Still, Mockers were a good choice for the honor.
They are ubiquitous around the state, but
don't congregate in huge noisy flocks
making messy nuisances of themselves,
as do sparrows, starlings, and grackles.
Mockers are as feisty as Texans, too,
giving no quarter to any creature
that violates their nesting territory.
I've seen a Mocker peck a cat bald
just for slinking near its nesting tree.
A pair of Mockers can harass a raptor
like kamikaze fighters buzzing a bomber.
But, of course, Mockingbirds are most renowned
for their mimicry of other birds' songs.
Their scientific name, *Mimus polyglottos*, means
"many languages." But it's a mystery why Mockers have
that ability. Surely it confers some survival benefit.
However, I've seen no scientific explanation for this trait.
Darwin, in his trip to the Galapagos Islands in 1835,
commented on how Mockingbirds varied in form,
island to island. This was one of the crucial facts
which led him to his Theory of Evolution.
But one would think that Mockers' mimicry of almost
any sound, as well as the songs of other birds,
would have impressed and intrigued him
even more than their physical variation.
Perhaps the mystery of the Mockingbird's mimicry
is another apt reason for making her the state bird.
Texas is certainly a land of mystery and contradiction.

Red-Tailed Hawk

One summer, during my early teenage,
I took the train from Fort Worth
to Amarillo to visit my cousin, Boyd,
on his family's chicken ranch in Dumas.
He and I spent many days exploring on foot
those high, dry plains of Texas' Panhandle.
It was a country of scrub brush, prickly pear,
and occasional puny mesquite trees,
far outnumbered by oil rigs, looking like
mechanical dinosaurs with obsessive, compulsive
disorder, pecking methodically at the earth.
Boyd and I spent many an imaginal hour
in that meager, unwelcoming environment,
finding rocks, and lizards to chunk them at,
and clouds cavorting amazing displays
of mythical creatures in that huge, hard sky.
Then we found something amazing:
a Red-Tailed Hawk's nest,
the size of a bassinet, woven intricately
from stems and grasses, and cunningly
hidden within a low, thorn-studded shrub.
It contained two fledglings, soft, plump,
and fluffy with just-formed feathers.
In another two weeks they would be trying to fly.
But we couldn't keep our hands off
these strange, magical creatures
with their fierce golden eyes
and clenching talons, sharp as
the thorns that guarded them.

We robbed them from their nest,
wrapped them in our shirts,
and took them triumphantly home.
We naively imagined to make them pets.
I even planned to take mine
back home on the train.
Boyd's father took them from us
and bashed them to bloody messes
near the chicken coops they might
have raided as adults.
Boyd and I were distraught

70

and I was outraged at this wanton
destruction of life and beauty.
I realized only much later, of course,
the sin was mine.
Now, as an adult, every time I see
a Red Tailed Hawk, soaring lordly
against the harsh, high Texas sky,
I remember that fierce-eyed fluff
I carried warm against my chest,
its heart thudding against mine
with innocent, obdurate trust,
and I begin, again, to understand.

Ode To The Texas Turkey Vulture

I have watched you squat on the shoulders,
awkward as broken umbrellas,
pretending to ignore, with strained
nonchalance, the fur-coated gore,
like a covey of nuns on holiday.
Ah, but I know why your heads are bald.
We can't have feathers catching, can we,
while dabbling in some armadillo's entrails?

You've adapted well to the altered ecology
of asphalt and automobiles.
You calculate just how long you can wait
before you must relinquish to a coming car.
Lifting, then, with leisurely flaps
of unflappable contempt, disdaining
any semblance of hurry, maintaining
your mortician's dignity.

But I fooled you once: chugging my old van
steady on, then, after you measured me, dismissively,
floored the accelerator!
Your head sprang like a jack-in-the-box,
beady eyes bloating in panic,
flapping frantically, knowing, though,
you couldn't get up in time.
I punched the brakes just before
you'd have splattered my windshield.
We were both quite abashed (and grateful
to be unbashed) by that foolishness.

Yes, I've ridiculed your clumsy pomposity
on the ground, but, of course,
that is not your element.
Soaring wide-winged in the heat shafts
above the lake and on the up-drafts
from the hills, you are, quite simply, magnificent.

You shear so close to our treetop deck,
I hear your wings' *Aeolian* arpeggios
as they harrow the heavy air.
Do you regard me an intruder in your aerie,

or as just a potential meal?
You've fed well enough from us;
we early accepted your disposal service,
since you seem to have the local monopoly.
And we've had few complaints.

But Mom was right surprised to find you
roosting on the deck rail that young summer morn.
Your fetid breath and reeking feathers
rather freaked her out. She shrieked and fell
to the deck; you hissed and fell to the sky.
Are the mighty, then, fallen to the stealing
of garbage? Or have you never been proud?

You scanned these canyons long before the lake.
You ranged the prairies with the Comanche,
descried the bison moving in a million
mindless waves of muscle, hoof, and horn
that roiled the earth
and boiled up dust to each horizon.

You witnessed the Indians worship
the herd with arrow and spear,
spilling the blood scent on the wind.
You were of that sacred way of life,
of the pure hardness of it.
You hissed the coyotes from your share
and gleaned the bright bones quickly bare.

In that time you were a nomad, too,
nestless, scribing far spirals.
You shall not feel again the bison's
thunder in your feathers
nor hunt with the gaunt riders.
Yet, it is you who have survived.
Indeed, these are your halcyon days,
for now the prairie is a tracery
of hardened arteries which bleeds
each day to keep you fat and numerous,
no longer nomads.

You lay your eggs among the stones
but gorge your chicks on possum bones.

Though accidently, unceremoniously slain,
the service is good by truck, car, or train.
Still, despite your new affluence,
you vaguely ache for the ancient way,
for the sacred confluence
of predator, scavenger, and prey.
Perhaps it will be so again someday.
As long as there is death, there's hope.
You've always found a way to cope.
For what is sacred in a way of life—
is it the life or the way?

Rattler

Bent like humble suppliants we press
through tangled cedar saplings and wild plum,
so white plum petals sprinkle us
like holy water shook from an aspergillum.

The dry creek canyon we tread collects
the blossoms' fragrance to cloyance,
as a cathedral immersed
in ceremony's pungent incense.

Where leaves and limbs allow, sun shafts
wander these shadowed chambers,
warm the sleeping stone so the aroma
of plum may hide the odor of us strangers.

The creek-way ends in a curved stone cliff,
as a triptych for an altar bathed in light,
where on its central sunlit ledge coils
a rattlesnake, huge and ancient anchorite.

He raises then his heavy head
swollen with a winter's venom.
Through the rocks he feels our tread,
desecrating his sanctum sanctorum.

With twin-tined quivers of his tongue
he tastes us amid the plum-thick air,
tastes our sweat, our steel, our fear,
knows us and does not move or seem to care.

But now the old one's head arises,
like a priest he makes a sign.
He is coiled upon the altar
with his yellow eye on mine.

His tongue flicks a benediction
as it trembles there in space
and he sighs with satisfaction
gliding slowly toward my face.

Now the rasping buzz of his rattle
like the snarl of a snare drum's roll
freezes mind and blood
with fear to the very soul.

And now his mouth has opened
and the fangs unfold, distend;
a drop of venom near escaping
as he hisses his amen.

Then his head jerks, torn to tatters
and he falls back to the rock.
Only then do I hear the gun
and feel its angry shock.

And my soul rises up within and asks:
What is this that I have done?
Have I killed some holy creature?
What unending here has now begun?

The Copperhead

I could not kill the copperhead
    that coiled upon my path.
Instead I killed the urge to kill
    which struck with fear-fanged wrath.
I can't say why I stayed my hand
    when fear and anger caught my breath,
Yet let them both subside and thought
    "I hold this creature's life or death."
It lay upon a flat raised rock
    in a single shaft of morning sun.
And it glistened red and gold and gray,
    seeming unaware that I was come.
Transfixed by its intense passivity,
    I let relax my mind and hand
And now with an empathic eye
    saw all its innocence and beauty.
Illumined in the gloom, it glowed,
    a bright corona, a sovereign's coronet.
Its cold and golden eye surveyed a realm
    man lost and would foolishly forget.
I could not kill the copperhead,
    but now it seems not odd;
Perhaps we must see all life sacred
    if we would reach for God.

Horned Frog

Not really a frog, of course,
but made famous with that name
as mascot of TCU's football team,
which finally had a winning season
about the time the Horned Toad,
(it's not a toad either, but a lizard),
became an endangered species due to unfair
competition from Fire Ants for the lizard's
primary food source, the Red Harvester Ant,
and from human usurpation of the dry
plains of Texas, the lizard's native habitat.
As a youngster I often carried these docile
little dinosaurs in my pocket, where they
would snuggle down for a nap until placed
on a Red Ant mound, where they would avidly
lunch on those brave but hapless hoards.
Neither fast nor large, the toads can puff up
their round little bodies to present a spinney
mouthful to a coyote or cat and, for further
discouragement, can squint blood from their eyes.
I miss my thorny little friends and hope
they will come back from near extinction,
even if it means my TCU team returns to mediocrity.

Catfish Skinning

The North Central plains of Texas
between Glen Rose and Stephenville
are accustomed to mild aridity.
Cedars are the climax vegetation,
efficiently finding and retaining
scarce ground water from the deep table,
competing even with prickly pear
for the bouldered hills, exceptions
to the sea floor's subsidence
during the Cretaceous Period.
Fossils of marine creatures: trilobites,
ammonites, mussels, spiral snails,
like hard, white ghosts,
haunt these desiccated hills,
still listening for the sea.
One hundred million years
they have waited for water.

But this is not desert.
Most years there is sufficient rain
to tantalize poor hopeful humans
into staying put, perhaps even raising
a few more cows or sheep.
Goats will thrive but are hard to keep.
Two years ago Frank stocked
his largest tank with channel catfish,
chummed them with corn,
and bet on rain like roulette in Vegas.
But we watched the tank circle shrink
from week to week, the water plundered
by thunder heads passing, teasing,
cackling with laughter as they
slid around the hills; one joke Johnnies
with their dry humor.

Finally, the tank was just
a large shallow puddle,
roiling with slick black fish
fighting for the deepest few inches.
*We'll have to kill them all
in order to save them*, said Frank.
I had heard that said in Vietnam

under just as fishy circumstances.
The pond was too shallow
and the bottom too uneven for nets.
We scattered Rotenone on the water
to consume all the oxygen.
The fish came gasping to the surface,
doubly betrayed by life,
much like ourselves.

But the fish had their revenge.
We bagged them in burlap,
flapping and writhing,
and kept them moist in the pickup bed,
perhaps two hundred pounds
and seventy-five fish.
On a sheet of plywood
atop two metal drums
we arranged our abattoir.
This is how it's done:
Grasp the fish above the dorsal spine
but behind the pectorals,
the only secure hold on its slippery body,
struggling to stab us
with those poisoned stilettos.

And they were successful
about as often as we were.
The spines are like rapiers
they use expertly against each other
in vicious lake bottom duels.
My third fish caught me in the thumb,
the pain lancing up my wrist
like electric barbwire.
Rub some of his slime into the wound,
Frank suggested. *The fish are coated
with their own poison antidote.*
It did seem to help.
But after cleaning thirty fish in three hours
My hands were swollen, stiff,
and bloody with wounds.

Once the fish is securely gripped,
the spines can be broken with pliers.
Slit him open, then, from anus to chin
and scrape out the entrails.

Peel off the skin with pliers
(like ripping off old wallpaper).
Finally, slice off each fillet
and toss the head and bones away.
But the catfish, tenacious
as any creature yet evolved,
is still alive,
its unclothed bones still undulating,
its open mouth and gills still gasping,
its cold, black eye still seeking mine.

Texas Tranquility

Mustangs

Horses are special animals.
Their domestication helped humans become
a more special, more dominant, species.
Horses, unlike most other domestic non-pets,
almost always are given names.
I've had a plentitude of horses in my life,
though I don't consider myself a real horse person.
I remember being astride my uncle's feisty Shetland,
name now forgotten, when I was about eight.
Granddad rode a regal palomino named Pal.
He taught me to ride on a gentle roan mare named Sally.
My sister-in-law's favorite, a pinto,
appropriately named Warrior,
tried to throw me thru a barbed-wire fence
just because I wasn't her.
My other sister-in-law, has an old, sweet,
one-eyed sorrel named Penny,
that my eight-year-old grandson loves to ride.
My daughter worked her way thru college
as a veterinary assistant whose
proudest vet accomplishment
was the castration of country singer
Clint Black's prize stallion.
It was also she who, at age 13,
was fence slashed while bareback riding
the neighbor's piebald filly.
Maybe it just runs in the family.

A mere 100,000 years ago, wild horses, *Equus ferus*,
were native and numerous in North America,
but they went extinct about 10,000 years ago, due,
they say, to the end of the last ice age, or, perhaps,
predation by Siberian nomads who wandered into
a continent devoid of other human inhabitants.
I'd like to think it wasn't the early Indians that killed
off those horses, since they would have been too
valuable for exploring, hunting, and warring.

Iberian horses played a major role in the Spanish
conquest of Mexico in the 1500's. But when
some became *mesteño*, "strayed livestock,"

they quickly reverted to feral animals, adapted
well to the vast Southwestern prairies, and multiplied
prodigiously to become wild mustangs:
mounts for vaqueros, cowboys, soldiers,
and, indeed, became the salvation
of Native Americans for 300 halcyon years,
so Indians were able to harrow and hallow
the buffalo herds from Texas to the far Dakotas.

Mustangs transformed the Comanche, Apache,
Kiowa, Cheyenne, Pawnee, and Sioux from
powerless pedestrians into mystic warriors
of the plains, the greatest horsemen the world has known,
and for whom horses became their medium of exchange,
their means of livelihood, the center of their art and culture.
For Anglos, mustangs made possible the adventuring,
soldiering, and ranching that conquered the western continent.

Now the Texas prairie has become fenced pastures,
cotton patches, cedar breaks, and oil fields.
Pickups have replaced horses
as the primary beast of burden.
But the hills and prairies and the horses remain,
perhaps dimly remembering in boulders and bones
when the great West was horse country
and when mustangs in their millions,
flowed across the plains as rivers
of Rococo flesh, perhaps more varied
in color and pattern than any other animal,
exuberant in their freedom and magnificent
in their perfect embodiment of those wilder,
more wondrous times.
I hope they keep running in my family.

Longhorns

Watching the daily cattle drive
at Fort Worth's Stockyards,
I enjoy seeing the placid longhorns
plodding up the red brick street,
the cowpokes cracking their whips
for the tourists rather than the cattle.
Those wonderful beasts are impressive,
even to a native Texan.

Texas might have been more aptly named
Longhornia or maybe Longhornland.
Spanish cattle ran wild in Texas from
the early 1500's, finding the hot, dry prairie
similar to their native Iberian plains,
and becoming Texas' dominant critter
for the next four centuries.
Longhorns can thrive on sparse grass and prickly pear,
can survive drought, dust, blizzards, and blasting heat,
have hides impervious to Mesquite thorns,
negotiate rocky *arroyos* with hard, sharp hoofs, and
wield their meter length horns like mounted lancers.

They are lanky, long-legged, wary and wily;
drop healthy calves with no help needed.
Their ability to fend for themselves on the open
range but herd together docilely for drives to market
gave rise to mythic cowboy culture and million-acre
ranches, to trailing them north on the Chisholm and
the Goodnight-Loving Trails to railroads in the East.

With the taming of the West, softer folk sought
fatter beef, so fewer rangy longhorns were wanted.
Ranches were fenced-in to fatten-up heavier cattle.
Longhorns nearly went extinct by the 1920's when
the few remaining longhorns were given refuge in
Texas state parks, to keep the breed alive.
Maybe now that leaner beef is viewed as healthier,
Longhorns will once again become more than
mere curiosities, and Texas will once again become
Longhornland.

Buffalo

I have a vivid memory from an auto trip as a child,
of looking up through the backseat window
of our '56 Chevy to see a herd of buffalo
stampeding to the edge of a mesa
and stopping there to look down on me.
Perhaps it was only a dream.

But I have always been fascinated by the lore
of buffalo herds, massed in their millions,
causing earthquakes and dust storms with their rampage,
pursued by horse-backed Indians shooting arrows
and thrusting spears into those enormous
misshapen bodies galloping at 40 miles an hour.
Bulls could whirl and gore with horns,
hefting horse and rider off the ground,
could leap their one ton mass six feet into the air,
could trample anything in their path.
And when the spring rains came to the prairie,
wildflowers sprang up to extend
a many-colored carpet to every horizon, because
the herds had scarified and pounded in the hard seeds.

Perhaps I was reading Parkman's *Oregon Trail*
when I dreamed I saw the buffalo herd on the butte.
He lived with the plains Indians, hunted buffalo with them,
described how each part of the animal was used
as food, tools, art, clothing, medicine, and shelter;
nothing wasted, and thanks to the Great Spirit,
Wakan Tanka, for the bounty of the hunt.

But when the railroads came to cross the plains,
the buffalo and the Indians were done for undoing.
The buffalo were resented for blocking the tracks,
were shot by the millions from the trains and left to rot.
The Indians' resistance to the relentless westward push
of white civilization was broken, not by cavalry or superior
weapons, but by massacre of the buffalo herds to deprive
the Indians, not just of food, but of their sacred way of life.
We commemorated them ironically by picturing
the Indian on the penny and the buffalo on the nickel.

Only a few hundred buffalo were left
by the end of the 19th century.
They were nurtured in national parks and private ranches,
so today they again number some thousands.
But perhaps the Great Spirit
is still with the Indians and the buffalo.
The Indians cling to the legend
of White Buffalo Calf Woman,
a mysterious maiden who transformed herself
into a white buffalo calf and promised
to come again to raise up the Indians to power.

Perhaps it is only a dream,
but with climate change turning West Texas
once again to arid plains, unfit for farming,
perhaps the buffalo and the Indians
will reclaim this territory as their natural birthright,
their sacred ground, so once again,
there will be the thunder of the herd
and the ululations of the painted riders.
But, then again, perhaps it is only a magnificent dream.

Black Jack

Jackrabbits have a well-
deserved bad reputation.
Their meat is tough and stringy,
which is fortunate
because they harbor
several kinds of disease-bearing
ticks, fleas, and vermin.
In African American folk tales,
Jackrabbit is a trickster god.
Hence the *Br'er Rabbit* tales
of Uncle Remus that Disney
made famous in *Song of the South*.
Jack is not really even a rabbit, but a hare.
Jacks are bigger, faster,
and nest on the ground, rather than
underground like regular rabbits.
Jacks' young are born sighted,
furred, and ready to ramble.
The name "Jack" refers to their huge ears,
which resemble those of the Jackass.
The ears not only give Jack extraordinary
hearing, but radiate body heat to keep him cool.
The Black-Tailed Jack of Texas
was said by Apache legend
to have started a fire
that burned Coyote blind,
but Jack then restored his eyes
if Coyote agreed not to hunt Jack.

That story almost recapitulated
on Frank one spring evening.
He had a camp fire going
on the back 40 near a fishing pond.
As he came back toward the fire
with a fish to fry, there was a Jack
with a glint in his eye,
and his ears riding high.
Seeing Frank, the Jack commenced
to jumping crazy-like, and actually
bounded thru the campfire,
sending sparks into the dry grass

that immediately caught fire
and came for Frank
on a following breeze.
Frank took to the pond
till the grassfire died,
then he stomped back up the hill
to douse the campfire.
His wet boots slipped
on the burned grass and he took
a tumble that left him covered in soot.
When he finally put out the fire
and began the walk homeward,
there was old Jack on the trail snickering.
"If my gun hadn't got wet,
I'd of had rabbit stew
instead of fish that night," Frank claimed.
But I've got my doubts.
Black Jack is just too tricky.

Turtle-Rabbit

is what the Aztecs called him,
because he has the shell
of a turtle but can run about quickly
and leap like a rabbit.
To us he is the armadillo,
the "little armored one."
We mostly see him smushed
on the road due to his instinct
to jump straight up when alarmed.
That's a good defense against
everything except an onrushing car.

Though we Texans like to brag
of bigness, we are lucky to have some
of the smaller breeds of dillo.
Down in South America
dillos can get up to 130 pounds,
and could probably damage
a car with their leaping.
Dillos have also gotten a bad rap
as being carriers of leprosy.
We shouldn't blame them, though,
the Spanish gave leprosy
to the Turtle-Rabbit while also
whupping up on the Aztecs.
Too bad the Aztecs didn't have
armor like dillos and the Spanish.

It's also too bad dillos love
to eat grub worms, because grubs
are what we *homo sapiens suburbous*
are most successful at cultivating
just beneath our luxuriant green lawns.
Dillos attack at dawn,
sniffing out the grubs,
just trying to be helpful
by digging them up,
and slurping them down.
But they don't replace the divots,
so we hunt them ruthlessly

for their sacrilege against
our most sacred ground.

My neighbor asked me to help
catch a dillo that was regularly
ravaging his magnificent lawn.
He had found the dillo's burrow
and he wanted me to lie in wait
near it to grab the dillo by the tail
as neighbor drove dillo to burrow.
It worked like a charm until
the dillo neared the hole.
I must have made some small noise,
for the dillo's ears twitched,
she came to an abrupt halt,
and, just as I lunged for the tail,
she leaped straight up a yard in the air
like a running back in traffic,
came down on top of me, and tried
to dig a new burrow thru my body.
I screamed and leaped into the air myself,
allowing dillo to disappear
into her hidey hole.

I haven't spoken with the neighbor
since the levitation incident.
The dillo has been staying hidden,
but I think she's still around.
I've read they produce identical
quadruplet pups about the time
the grass greens up in the spring.
I put in a gravel lawn this winter,
so my neighbor has all those
juicy gorging grubs in his.
Oh, *schaden-freude,*
thy name is Dillo.

Old Snort

Frank was driving his rusty ranch pickup
one evening from the house,
along the half-mile dirt driveway,
to his rural route mail box.
He was almost there when
he encountered a sounder
of wild pigs crossing the road.
He managed to halt the pickup,
which had been clipping along
at five miles an hour, but
whose brakes were nearly extinct.

The pigs stopped too,
and turned to gaze at Frank
with some expectancy, it seemed to him.
This was the largest sounder
he had ever seen; must have been
over twenty pigs, large and small.
He had stepped out of the truck
to take a picture when he heard
the distinct grinding rasp
of whetters on cutters from behind him.
A huge hog with vicious curved tusks
was easing toward him from the rear,
a classic flanking maneuver
General Patton would have been proud of.
Having been a high-jumper in school,
Frank managed to back-flip
into the bed of the pickup
just before the hog would have
knocked him down and invited
the troop to have him for supper.
Wild pigs are opportunistic omnivores;
they eat anything and everything,
leaving nothing.
Frank had noticed that the rattlesnake
population on his ranch had declined
as the pigs proliferated.
Frank guessed why
the pigs were riled up now.
For weeks he had been feeding them
their favorite snack, fermented corn,

near a hunting blind.
He wanted to shoot some pigs,
or capture a few for butchering.
But that had gotten too expensive,
so he had ceased feeding a few days ago.
Frank had read up on wild pigs
and knew they are quite intelligent.
But he hadn't realized they could
hold a grudge like this.
Old Snort, as Frank immediately
denominated the immense boar,
put his front trotters up on
the pickup's running board.
His weight caused the pickup to lean
precariously toward him,
the springs being long since spavined.
Snort's back hairs bristled
in the infamous razorback pattern
inherited from imported European boars
that had mated with the domestic pigs,
which had escaped from the Spaniards
during their settlement of Mexico and Tejas.
Snort was definitely irritated.
His little red eyes found Frank's frightened blues.
Frank could also smell creosote on the hog
that came from the pig's habitual
rubbing against telephone poles.
Snort bellowed for Frank to come out
and fight like a pig.
He scraped his tusks along the scrim
of rust that separated them.
Frank politely declined.
The indignant Snort, his point made,
rejoined his chortling herd,
and they disappeared into gathering dusk.
The next day Frank found
his fenced garden pig-ravaged,
and decided the better part of valor
was to recommence providing the pigs
their fermented corn.
That's when Frank realized
he had been transporting
several sacks of corn in the pickup bed
the day of the porcine assault.

So, probably Old Snort was simply
trying to get at the corn.
But Frank ruefully entertained
the alternative possibility
that the hog would have climbed
into the driver's seat
if Frank had left the door open,
and the whole sounder might then
have migrated to more propitious pastures.

Dinosaurs

I've loved dinosaurs all my life.
my dad studied historical geology
in college and I was fascinated by
his textbook on the subject,
which showed pictures of dinosaurs
and described their lives and times
hundreds of millions of years ago.
Dad and I often went searching for fossils
in local creeks and rock formations.
We found Ammonites, Trilobites,
and other ancient sea creatures
from the Mid-Cretaceous, when Texas
was covered by a shallow sea
that split North America down the middle.
But before and after that period, land dinosaurs,
such as *Tyrannosaurus Rex*, *Triceratops*,
and the Texas State Dinosaur, *Paluxysaurus*,
roamed Texas and gave their bones for fossils
paleontologists are excavating today.
I avidly read science-fiction stories about
time-traveling back to the era of dinosaurs.
I would love to see them alive.
Perhaps, someday, science will have advanced
enough that time-travel to see dinosaurs
will be possible, or DNA replication will allow
dinosaurs to be recreated as envisioned
by such movies as Jurassic Park.
Dinosaurs reigned for 200 million years.
Humans have been around only half a million,
yet we are already on the verge of extinction.
Half a century after my infatuation
with dinosaurs, my grandsons continue
that love affair. We peruse illustrated books
displaying the vast variety of dinosaurs,
now showing they often had feathers
and mottled, multi-hued hides,
the beauty of which only their large-
brained successors can admire
and be astonished by.
I wonder if humans will be considered
beautiful or interesting by whichever

species succeeds us in Earth's future?
We will likely be extinguished, not by some
accidental meteor, but by our own misuse
of these large but, maybe not large enough,
brains we are so proud of, and with which
we both ridicule and romanticize the dinosaurs.
Will we even be noticed a few million years
hence, when our cities, arts, and bodies
are but dust? We will not be preserved
like the dinosaurs. We will be but an eye blink,
perhaps unrecorded in Earth's panorama of life.
An intelligent successor species
will probably again marvel at the dinosaur
fossils they will find and will wonder
what mysterious catastrophe occurred
to destroy so many species in our mere human
moment of geologic time 65 million years after
the magnificence of the dinosaurs.

Texas *Ars Poetica*

Not exactly a Texas Critter,
but included because it's the Texas State Tree

Poetry should seek to emulate
the humble Texas pecan: lying in wait
for the patient seeker to find her,
this errant armored wanderer.
Her plain, sleek, solid shell
(unassumingly elegant sartorial),
mottled with subtle abstraction,
(a whole tree in its act of creation),
takes polish from a caring hand,
is resistant to naïve demand,
yields treasure to clever tenacity,
a nugget of nutritious veracity.
So give the Texas pecan poem a whirl,
and hope it won't fall to some idiot squirrel.

Part IV: Texas Folks

Zuni Pueblo

Basket

It's about the right size to hold a human heart.
And as I hold it in my hands,
the little basket, I mean,
it seems to pulse like a living heart
when I gently press its
lightning-patterned bulbous base.
Woven tight from yellow and brown
Texas tall-prairie grasses
by a name-lost Lakota woman,
grown old in Texas, though
in her youth roamed Dakota's Black Hills,
(perhaps even Crazy Horse's
lost daughter, who was said
to have married white and moved South).
She would have been about the right age,
my great grandmother.

Persisting in anonymous elegance,
the basket has no maker's label or mark,
no indication of origin beyond its simple
perfection of design, embodying some
ten thousand woven years of work.
It was meant, perhaps, to hold
healing herbs or berries,
but for some reason was never used,
a virgin vessel, unstained
by what it would have otherwise contained.

So the little basket came down to me
through generations of caring family,
always pristine and empty,
except, of course, for the human heart
its ancient art so lovingly contains.

Kite Kin

My father, an aircraft engineer
at General Dynamics, Fort Worth,
loved to build and fly paper kites.
When I was ten he constructed
a magnificent box kite
taller than I, and as empty of experience.
I painted it with bright crimson lacquer.

We hiked the kite up a nearby hill
whose ridge always held breeze.
Dad gave me the kite to hold, then
backed away, unwinding the string
from a fishing reel.
At his signal I ran and loosed the kite,
an offering to the wind.
It floated up like bubble,
red as a kiss for the sky.

We flew it for an hour,
teaching it tricks with fancy pulls,
then reeled it reluctantly to earth.
Next day, with Dad at work,
I took the kite alone to the hilltop.
It soared up like an eager young eagle,
higher than the day before.
We both exalted in our freedom and power.

Then the wind gusted fiercely
from the storm I hadn't noticed.
String sizzled against my fingers
as I tried to keep the kite from leaping away.
In pain and surprise, as if a friend
had slashed me with a knife,
I released the string and the kite disappeared.

Dad was angry, not so much
at the loss of the kite as at my foolishness.
But he quickly calmed and reassured me

with his gentle humor that it was better
to have lost the kite than for me
to be a mile above Texas
headed north with a flock of geese.

This all comes back to me
so many years later,
as the father of a teenage girl,
her hair as red as that errant kite.
She seems to embody its spirit,
so beautiful, wild, and innocent.
She's burned my fingers many times,
but I hope I'm wise enough now
to know when to let go.

Rapid Evolution

Frank's ranch near Stephenville, Texas

Driving the half-mile ranch road from house to mail box,
Frank stops the pickup abruptly and prematurely.
"Will you look at that!" he growls, exiting the truck,
slamming the door so hard the rusty hulk rings like a bell.
"Those dipwit dogs passed right by it and didn't even notice."
Attempting to defend the dogs, I say, "Now, Frank,
you know Buster hasn't been worth much since he caught
that high fly baseball between the eyes,
and Prissy is probably on the scent of a rabbit or something."
"Well, it would certainly get their attention if they got nailed."
The three-foot long rattler lies stretched out straight
on the dirt road, long and plump, absorbing the warmth
of an early autumn's late afternoon.
"You see he's not coiled and didn't rattle," says Frank.
"That's forced, rapid evolutionary behavior change if you ask me.
The ones that rattle get killed off quicker,
leaving those less prone to rattle to mate and procreate.
The dogs' instinct is probably to key on the coil and rattle.
They probably don't even notice the snake otherwise."
He finds a mesquite branch and pins the snake at the neck.
Then slipping out a well-honed, homemade blade,
he knifes the snake through the head and hoists
the writhing body to the tail gate of the truck.
"I usually don't bother to skin 'um,
but there's a cute little Chinese gal up at the college,
asked me to bring her snake meat and skins."
He slices off the head and begins to make
a delicate incision down the middle of the belly.
I hold the tail, keeping the body taut
to aid his long straight cut.
As the last third of its length bursts open,
about a dozen three-inch snakelets come wiggling
from its innards, hissing and striking at the knife.
Frank jumps back, dropping his end of the mother snake,
sending the body swinging back toward me
leaking guts and enraged snake babies.
I yelp and dodge, slinging the body ten feet away.

Several of the little ones slip quickly into the grass
as we wildly stomp those still hissing on the road.
Frank tentatively retrieves the mother snake's body
and finishes flensing the skin. "You know," says Frank,
"we may be in trouble if forced rapid evolution works
for those little bastards. I'd sure hate to be responsible
for a race of flying rattlesnakes."

Bass Reeves Heading Out

Granddad Was A Cowboy

When I was ten I spent a summer with him
on his ranch in Denver City, Texas.
It was a real adventure for this city boy.
He taught me to ride a horse and use a lasso
(though not the two in combination).
I practiced roping fence posts and chairs,
most anything that would hold still.
We would ride together for hours,
supposedly checking fence and rounding strays,
but I think he mostly enjoyed the peacefulness
of the prairie and the bleak beauty of it.
It was all exotic to me: Cactus, Mesquite, Sagebrush,
Tumbleweed, Yucca, Cedar, inter-sprinkled
with wildflowers, thriving in spite of drought
and sun-scorch from a relentless sky.

One day we drove a few cattle into a corral.
He showed me how to tail-twist a cow
into a squeezer machine to be injected
with serum to keep them healthy.
I wanted to see how they were branded,
but that had been done back in the spring.
He asked me if I wanted to try bull riding.
I would have said yes to just about anything cowboy.
He lassoed a yearling calf and held it down
while I got on, told me to hang tight, then let it go.
I was on the ground about five seconds later,
having spent two of those in the air.
When I caught my breath, I was ready to go again,
but he said it might ruin the calf for rodeo.
I had bought my first pair of boots for this visit.
They came in handy for more than just riding.
While walking thru a pasture one evening,
we got too close to a rattlesnake.
He heard the whirr of the snake's rattles,
and jerked me back just as it struck,
recoiling off my boot. It was a small specimen,
or else might have caught me above my boot.

He always carried a pistol, and quickly dispatched
the unlucky varmint. I was more excited than scared.
He suggested it wouldn't be necessary to mention
the incident to my Mom and Dad.

When my parents picked me up to return home,
Granddad presented me with a Winchester 22 rifle.
It had a rare octagon shaped barrel,
and was five times older than myself.
He said he often used it to shoot coyotes from horseback.
I loved that gun and hunted rabbits with it myself.
A few years later Granddad visited us
and borrowed the rifle for a hunting trip.
I never saw it or him again.

Moon of Popping Trees

In the moon of popping trees,
when ice glazed branches break
like gun shots or shake glistering shards
upon the bare night prairie,
when the wind voices beckon,
I wrap my bones in a buffalo robe
and crunch across the ground frost,
my feathers pointing the way
to Bear Hump hill, the vision place,
where I may step out of myself,
to become an antlered shaman
of ancient times, to see
the green boughs blossom with fruit,
and bison, elk, and antelope mingle
in numberless herds, invoking
our worship, providing our plenty.
But these are now just restless ghosts,
almost invisible within
the belly of the night,
upon the trackless white,
and there is really nothing here
but the bone white moon,
the dumb white snow,
the cold white wind of time.

Last Hunt

Frank owns a prime Texas hunting ranch,
but he quit hunting several years ago.
When I asked why, he told me this tale:
He built a deer blind of hay bales against
the barb wire fence of his lower pasture.
Before dawn he set up in the blind with
a good view of the woods from which
the deer would emerge to graze.
The only other occupant of the pasture
was his prized red Angus bull, Bruser.
The inquisitive bull came up and snorted
at Frank in the blind. Frank waved at Bruser
to shoo him away, to which Bruser replied
by pissing copiously toward the blind.
Frank threw a stone at Bruser, and the bull
obligingly sauntered off. A while later,
a couple of deer eased into the field warily.
Frank got one in the focus of his gun scope,
leading the now trotting deer by a foot or so.
But just as he pulled the trigger, the deer
veered off and the bullet just grazed it.
Frank found the deer in his scope once more
when the image of Bruser suddenly appeared,
huge and stupid in the scope's crosshairs,
not twenty feet away.
Frank jerked up the gun, losing the deer,
but saving Bruser from becoming
hamburgers, at least for the time being.
Fully frustrated, Frank walked toward
the house still grumbling about the bull.
Then a rafter of wild turkeys materialized
about twenty-five yards away, gobbling
and strutting and bobbing their heads
like a gaggle of church ladies all a gossip.
Frank had five bullets in his deer rifle
and says to himself, "If I hit one in the body
there won't be nothing left, but since they're
all bunched together, I can probably get one
if I shoot at all those heads." So he fired

all five shots through their bobbing, weaving,
beady-eyed babbling, only to see the whole
flock hurry away with an indignant flurry of feathers.
Thoroughly disgruntled, Frank continued
toward the house wondering how he could have
missed the turkeys. Now the wounded white-tail
made his reappearance, giving Frank the gimlet eye
from near enough for Frank to have hit the deer by
throwing his empty rifle at it. But Frank just
sighed and vowed that this would be his last hunt.

Lone Star Heritage

Sam Houston

was a big man. The biggest man in Texas
during his life, and I think always will be.
He was probably not as big as his statue
that seems to stand in the middle
of Highway I-45 at Huntsville,
dominating the landscape impressively.

But he probably looked that big when
he scared the crap out of the Mexican army
at San Jacinto, April 21, 1836,
as he rode at the head of his Texian troops,
arrayed in a single long line to make their
outnumbered force seem larger.
The Twin Sisters' throats belched fire
into the Mexicans' fortified camp,
its inhabitants mostly in siesta.
The furious Texian infantry roared in unison:
"Remember the Alamo!" and "Remember Goliad!"

Houston loomed over ten feet tall
on his silver war stallion, Saracen.
His sabre flashed fearsome in the mid-day sun.
He had two horses shot from beneath him,
and suffered a shattered ankle,
but he led his rag-tag Texians to total victory
while losing only a handful, and captured
General/President Santa Anna in his underwear.
It was one of the most monumental battles
in world history, making possible acquisition
of America's great western frontier.

Houston is often compared to George Washington,
and rightly so. They both won despite
overwhelming odds. Sam was the only officer
both charismatic enough to keep his troops' trust
and canny enough to outmaneuver
an enemy superior in numbers, in firepower,
and in military discipline.

Like Washington too, Sam was the only man
seriously considered to become first President
of the newly formed Republic of Texas.

He acquitted that office twice with distinction.
It was also Sam who brought Texas to statehood,
and Sam who, as Texas' Governor, vainly
tried to keep the state out of the Civil War.
That was his only major failure as a statesman,
but it proved his wisdom, courage, and nobility.
Houston is the biggest man in Texas history,
not least because he had to overcome
so many obstacles and personal misfortunes:
His first wife left him, causing him to resign
as Governor of Tennessee.
Had he stayed, he'd likely been elected
President of the United States.
His friend, President Andrew Jackson,
persecuted his adopted family, the Cherokee Indians.
Sam was often reviled as an Indian lover,
but saved many lives due to his treaties with them.
He struggled with alcoholism his entire life,
but never made a drunken mistake.
He never compromised his integrity
for political gain or anything else,
and lost many supporters because of it.
I believe Houston, while equally noble, was
an even better general and statesman than Washington.
Sam Houston will always be the biggest man in Texas.

Buffalo Soldiers

After the Civil War, Texas became even more
a cauldron of violence than before.
Outlaws, renegades, and disgruntled rebels
descended on Texas in hoards.
Conflicts between ranchers and farmers boiled.
Mexico seethed at Texas' southern border.
Indians marauded in violent despair
at the overwhelming destruction of their culture.
The 9th and 10th U.S. Cavalry were sent into south Texas
to quell the unrest, to make it safe to settle.
These units were known as the Negro Cavalry by whites
but were called the Buffalo Soldiers
by their Indian opponents, because their kinky
black hair reminded Indians of the buffalo mane,
and because they fought with the ferocity of a cornered buffalo.
They were stationed various times between 1869 and the late 1870's
at Fort Clark, near Brackettville, Fort Concho, near San Angelo,
Fort Griffin, Fort Richardson, and Fort Davis. They ranged
throughout Texas and the West, fighting Indians, repelling
Mexican revolutionaries, and generally enforcing the peace.
They also built forts and roads, strung telegraph lines,
mapped unknown areas, protected the mail, rescued settlers.
They earned 9 Medals of Honor during the Indian Wars and
went on to fight with Teddy Roosevelt in Cuba,
with "Black" Jack Pershing in Mexico, and distinguished
themselves in all subsequent Wars as well.
But it was as Indian fighters that they gained their name
and their reputation for fierceness and valor.
Texas became settled and prospered in no small measure
due to the efforts of the Buffalo Soldiers,
who often bore Texans' scorn,
both for their race and for their blue uniform.
The buffalo above crossed sabers became
the symbol patch on their uniforms.
Their motto was "We can, we will." They could and they did.
The Buffalo Soldiers' exploits now have a proud and honored place
in Texas history. Perhaps their ghosts patrol our prairies still.

Texas Pioneer Women

Being mostly anonymous and unrecorded
during their time, they are little celebrated
in Texas history, those thousands of women
who came to Texas from the 1820's on,
to help *Tejas* become Texas.
I've often marveled at why ordinary women
would travel to that harsh, violent country
to make their homes and raise their families.

Texas was perhaps the most dangerous place
in North America to settle in the early 1800's.
The black land prairie resisted farming.
The weather was unpleasant in every possible way.
The Mexican government was inconsiderate
when not openly hostile. They mostly left that
to the encroached upon Indians:
Apache, Tonkawa, Kiowa, Kichai, Wichita,
and most especially, the Comanche,
who were the dominant tribe of west Texas,
always eager to rape, murder, and pillage
white settlers who invaded like locusts
competing for food, land, and way of life.

Because Texas was not a state until 1845,
there was little prior law or governmental force.
When the Civil war took the men away,
the women and children were left
to fend for themselves against all evils.
Thousands of Texas women and children
were captured by the Comanche
either to die or adapt to Indian life.
The few women who were rescued
after years of living as Indians,
usually preferred the Indian life
to the hardships of Anglo frontier settlers,
and often returned to the Indians.

A few women are lauded in Texas history
merely for being there, at Gonzales, the Alamo,
during the Runaway Scrape, and at San Jacinto,
but these were minor and even mythical roles

compared to the everyday hardships
women endured and sometimes survived
in those early years of the taming
and renaming of Texas.

There are few commemorations
of pioneer Texas women.
A statue at Texas Women's University in Denton
is dedicated to *The Texas Pioneer Woman.*
Created for the Republic's Centennial in 1935,
it shows only a lone standing woman
looking somewhat severe, left hand to her heart.
No tools or symbols of her station, no indication
of her struggles or accomplishments.
She is virtually obscured by hundreds of
flamboyant monuments around the state
to male heroes of the Texas Revolution,
to cowboys, soldiers, politicians.

The Texas Cowgirl Museum in Fort Worth
provides some scant recognition to pioneer women,
but emphasizes more the glamorous
ideals of Texas womanhood:
rodeo competitors, cowgirl movie stars,
and modern Texas women who benefitted
from the sacrifices and social capital
so painfully accrued by the early women settlers.

These were women who farmed and ranched,
hunted and herded, fought Indians and illnesses,
endured blasting heat, frigid cold, dust storms,
tornados, drought, flood, scouring winds,
wild beasts, breach births, broken bones,
death of husbands and children, loneliness.
How and why they triumphed over such
adversities is an enigma of our humanity.
And yet, the women probably would not
consider it such.
They looked upon the land
they had been brought to
and simply set to work to civilize it,
to impart some beauty into its harshness,

to sink roots and care and flesh into its soil,
to find a way to love it,
to make it home.

Michael Baldwin holds masters degrees in Library Science and Political Science. He retired in 2014 from a career as a library administrator and professor of American Government. His poetry book, *Scapes*, won the Eakin Poetry Book award, 2011, and his chapbook, *Counting Backward From Infinity*, won the Morris Memorial Chapbook award, 2012. He is also the author *of Murder Music*, a mystery-thriller novel, and *Passing Strange*, a collection of Science-Fiction short stories.

A native Texan, Johnny Bowen now lives in the rural Ozarks. In 2006, he retired as a consulting engineer to devote his time to painting. Bowen's oil painting methods range from highly detailed, brushmark-free landscapes and still lifes to more impressionistic palette knife paintings.

CPSIA information can be obtained
at www.ICGtesting.com
Printed in the USA
FSOW03n1216070616
21222FS

9 781942 956143